I0412149

The BRITISH

Reverence towards Nationality

(synopsis)

Towards Britain's 2016 Referendum
on Membership in the EU

YEHUDA COHEN

Priests
Publishing

Copyright © Yehuda Cohen, 2014.

The right of Yehuda Cohen to be identified as Author of this work has been asserted in accordance with the Copyright, Design and Patents Act 1988

First published as eBook in 2014 (Kindle)
Published in printed paperback in 2015 by
PRIESTS PUBLISHING
www.priestspublishing.com

All rights reserved. Except for the quotation of short passages for the purposes of criticism and review, no part of this publication may be reproduced, stored in a retrieval system, or transmitted, in any form or by any means, electronic, mechanical, photocopying, recording or otherwise, without the prior permission of the publisher.

ISBN: 978-965-90615-2-5 (eBook)
ISBN: 978-1-511-5275-5-2 (PB)

Typeset and designed by Priests Publishing
Printed by CreateSpace, an Amazon.com Company, Charleston SC

Contents

Introduction

This is the fifth in a series of volumes that seeks to analyze the European Union and its component groups from the perspective of national identity, and how self-ascription within the EU's member states – each the result of unique experiences – can be expected to impact on the future of the European Union.

The British are a collective with a political consciousness united by way of a unique constitution that dictates their organization and activities – a constitution which is, for the most part, unwritten. They are culturally and linguistically bound to other groups who share their Anglo-Saxon culture, while their ties to continental Europe are somewhat looser. The British Isles have traditionally been considered to be distinct from the continent, as exemplified in their legal system that employs Common Law. In addition, although part of the European Union (EU), the British refuse to adopt the euro as their currency and prefer to adhere to the traditional pound sterling on which currency their queen is depicted. This description of the British, however, is quite superficial since it disregards elements and historical developments which have, over many generations, defined what is unique about the British. The British shared a common history with the peoples of the continent, the advent of Christianity as religion supreme, the religious reformation, the Renaissance and the World Wars. Still, the British were uniquely and differently affected by those occurrences. One of the first concepts to which the Renaissance gave rise to throughout Europe (Britain included) was the ideal of the nation. Thanks to the Renaissance, the emergence of the nation-state system occurred. The various peoples of this society (the English, the French, the Spanish, the Italians and the Germans) had now moved from Christendom, with the pope and the emperor at their head, to the ideal of national identification, resulting in a change in the concept of Christendom that disunited Europe as European states began to succumb to nationalist feelings.

What was unique about the English political system (and, in consequence, the later British system) was not just the existence of Parliament as an institution that represented every section of English society. It was also the fact that their Parliament became stronger in the wake of events which broadened the base of its power and was an event peculiar to England. The English, followed by the Scots and the Welsh, lived in accordance with a political system which they themselves had evolved, a system in which increasingly broad segments of the public became involved in internal and external affairs and in imperial policy. They engendered a politically-aware populace interested in the management of imperial affairs. Thus British national identity gradually emerged, and the British adherence to their crown was the idea which defined their 'Britishness'. Since their history goes back nearly a millennium, and broad swathes of the public cherish the national myths of their heroes and venerable forefathers, the British national identity is built upon solid foundations.

In light of the previous surveys in this series, it would appear that Britain, in contrast to the Germans, the French, the Italians and the Dutch (but not the Spanish), did not join the European Union with its national identity in a fractured or extinguished state and are unlikely to prefer a European identity over their own national self-image. Britain's membership is based upon an Act of Parliament declaring that Parliament retains the right to abolish British membership. In this light, the British expressed their unwillingness to fully integrate with the European Union; this unwillingness is due to the strong, healthy and vibrant British national identity.

CHAPTER ONE

From Antiquity until 1485 CE

For close to a millennium, up to these very days, the British Isles have suffered no conquests by foreign enemies. British history is, however, riddled with invasions prior to 1000 CE: from the Romans, Saxons, Danes and Normans. These invasions, over time, have served to define the British nation and culture as we see it today.

The Romans

Romans were first recorded to have landed in Britain around 55 BCE. The then-Roman emperor, Julius Caesar, landed in the British Isles with a force of eight thousand soldiers, where he established an encampment. Julius Caesar fought a war with the Briton chieftain Cassivellanus and won, and thus Roman rule over Britain began. In 30 BCE, Augustus Caesar became the Roman emperor after the assassination of Julius. He brought about a system where by tribute-paying kings and princes ruled in Britain, enforcing one law and language (Latin) all through the Roman Empire. By 43 CE, Britain had become a part of the Roman Empire and remained until 410 CE. Scotland was, however, impossible to conquer; the Romans therefore constructed a line of fortifications on the Scottish border effectively separating Scotland from England. Roman Britain was therefore essentially divided into a mountainous part with fortified military camps and the plains containing Roman civilized cities and Romanized inhabitants therein.

Emergence of England

The Saxons arrived in Britain in the years 449–613 CE, alongside the Goths and Vandals: all Germanic tribes. The Anglo-Saxons gave the name *engla land* (the land of Angles) to the British lowlands. The years following the Anglo-Saxon invasion saw about a dozen kingdoms come into existence, which was later on reduced to seven and eventually to three. The Celts living in the conquered regions were relocated into northern and eastern England as well as Wales. By the end of the sixth century, the British population was half Celt and half Saxon (Anglo-Saxon). The culture by this time was predominantly Anglo-Saxon influenced.

The Church and English Nationality

A Note on Nationality:

It is important to draw distinctions between nationhood based on national identity and feelings, and ethnicity which nonetheless lacks the element of nationality. This distinction is addressed at length in our other volumes in this series about the groups which make up the European Union. Nationality is itself a myth; it is a spiritual state which a massive group of people adopts in connection with a vision of a link among members of the group and a belief in the myths which depict their own history to them, myths about their ancestors and, occasionally, also about struggles or enemies. Such myths give rise to a unique culture. Often, there is a religion or a specific sect within a re-ligion which had participated in the formation of the group and its culture. It is immaterial whether or not these myths are true or possess a kernel of truth, or whether it is possible to know if they are true or not, or even whether historical research proves them false. These concepts highlighted above only turn the group into an ethnicity. An ethnic group then becomes a nation if, in addition to all the aforementioned elements, it also aspires to sovereign rule or to participation in the sovereign rule of the territory to which the myths relate the group – a territory in which the whole group or part of it lives or aspires to live, a territory associated with an ancient myth according to which the group lived there in the past.

English nationality was greatly influenced by the advent of Christianity on the Isles. Towards the end of Roman rule in Britain, Christianity was adopted on the Isles; the Saxon invasion, however, successfully overcame Roman rule; Christianity inclusive. This occurred throughout the Isles of Britain, except for in certain areas of the west where Celtic groups managed to preserve their independence. These Celts had no connection to Rome and were attached to saints who were unknown on the continent, such as Saint Patrick. Saint Patrick was able, in his later years, to successfully disseminate the Christian faith. There were other notable saints who worked to bring the religion back to the Isles, like Saint Benedict of Italy (480–543 CE) and Saint Gregory the Great who even became elected to the papacy (590–604 CE), to mention a few. Roman missionaries completed the work of Christianizing Britain's southern and eastern provinces in the years 597–681 CE. In the seventh century, all of Britain, including Scotland and Wales, submitted to the pope's authority. In 668, the pope sent a Greek monk, Theodore of Tarsus, to organize and unify the English Church. He was appointed Archbishop of Canterbury and, for over twenty years, worked to organize the Church. He divided Church land into bishoprics and parishes, and established monasteries which served as religious centers. Every Christian was then required to dedicate a tithe of one-tenth or one-fifth of his produce to God. The Anglo-Saxon concepts of diocese, parish and tithe are still used today within the Church of England. According to Carter and Mears[1], these traditional divisions developed to form the English sense of nationality; in other words, these divisions shaped English unity and the English perception of themselves as a nation. Carter and Mears go on to relate that, in times when England was divided into a number of kingdoms, the English Church was the only force which unified all Englishmen. English unity, so they believe, was thus transformed into a single English entity as early as the period 400–600 CE, a process which continued to be reinforced throughout the following period until the tenth century CE and beyond. In the seventh, eighth, ninth and tenth centuries CE, wars among various kings in Britain took place; in which course Wales lost territory. A united English kingdom was later created under King Egbert of Wessex. This king remained on the throne until the Danish invasion that overwhelmed all the other existing rulers. Eventually, the heirs of Egbert, king of Wessex, defeated the Danes and reunited Anglo-Saxon England.

The Danes

The Danes (also called Vikings); seafarers originating in the fjords of Norway and the Danish peninsula, invaded England in the eighth century. Unlike in the time of the Anglo-Saxon invasion, the Danes did not suppress the local Anglo-Saxon religion or language. They ranged far and wide, first settling in Iceland, then later, under the leadership of Eric the Red, they explored Greenland and the coast of North America. They occupied the islands between Norway and Scotland, and from there continued to Ireland where they founded a number of cities, including Dublin. In his book, Green[2] notes that the Danes who arrived in the British Isles came from the peninsula in Denmark (today known as Jutland) formerly called Anglia. Thus their new place of settlement in Britain too came to be known as Anglia. They were uneducated rustics, but as freemen – not as the subjects of nobles – they bore arms which they used to defend themselves, and administered a rudimentary justice system based on an 'eye for an eye' and a 'life for a life'. As they settled in England, the concept of the freeman was replaced by that of the freeholder – whoever did not possess land was not considered free, even though he was not a slave.

Tacitus (the Roman historian who was the first to describe the English) depicted them as farmers and shepherds. They lived in villages whose independence they defended vigorously. Every village possessed common land and included families considered of noble blood, whose members were the leaders in times of war and peace. However, supreme authority lay with an

1 Carter, E. H., and R. A. F. Mears. *A History of Britain.* Oxford: Clarendon Press, 1937, 1946.
2 Green, John Richard. *A Short History of the English People.* London: Dent and Sons, 1962.

assembly of all landowners who convened from time to time near a holy tree, where they would conduct trials and determine the law in accordance with accepted custom. This institution would, in the course of time, give rise to the British Parliament. According to Carter and Mears, the Danes raided Britain, targeting its monasteries and burning a number of towns in England and Ireland. In 870, all of England, with the exception of Wessex, fell into their hands. Alfred, Egbert's grandson, ruled Wessex in the years 871–899 CE. In 878, the Danes launched a surprise attack on Alfred's army. The king extricated himself with difficulty and, together with a scant following, found temporary shelter through the winter on the moors of his kingdom, from where he directed the attacks of his supporters against the Danes. In an agreement signed in 878, Alfred and the Danish King Guthrum divided England between themselves, and the Danish king was baptized. Seven years later, Alfred was strong enough to impose a treaty upon the Danes in which his territory was enlarged; this came to include London, which he later fortified. Alfred's son overcame the Danes and became king of all of England.

The years 878–978 CE are considered the 'Golden Age' of the Anglo-Saxons. Although Alfred was king of only part of England (as were his ancestors) – namely, Wessex – his heirs ruled over all of England. The existence of such a 'Golden Age' is proof of progress that had a spiritual component, possibly due in part to the growing sense of national cohesion.

Alfred's grandson, Athelstan (925–940 CE), eliminated the last vestiges of Danish rule in England. He bore not only the title of King of England, but that also of King of Britain, having defeated and subjugated the kings of western Wales, Scotland, Monmouth and Northumbria. Alfred's great-grandson, Edgar the Peaceful (959–975 CE), regularly sought the counsel of Saint Dunstan. The latter was born into a well-to-do family. He loved music and was sent to the royal court – which proved not to his liking – so he entered a monastery. Dunstan later joined a group of itinerant Irish monks, occupied himself with learning and reading, and became a goldsmith. He moved to the court and, at the age of twenty, was appointed head of a monastery. He was a close friend of Edgar, the king's son. After Dunstan's death, England went through a period of wars and the monastic reform was abolished. Dunstan deserves much of the credit for the peace and prosperity during Edgar's undramatic reign.

In the reign of Edgar's son, Ethelred the Redeless (the Unready), the Danes returned once more to raid England and terrorize its cities. Ethelred imposed a heavy tax on his subjects in order to pay the Danes to stop their raids. The amount (which he paid in six installments) was the equivalent today of eight-and-a-half-million pounds sterling. At the same time, Ethelred tried, unsuccessfully, to defeat the Danes in battle, but the Danes prevailed. In 1014, Ethelred returned to England in order to liberate his kingdom from Danish rule, but two years later he too died, and his eldest son, Edmund 'Ironsides', became king and organized an army in East Anglia. This army was defeated in 1016 by Canute, the new Danish king, following an act of betrayal by an English baron. The defeat was not complete, however, and therefore the two kings agreed to divide England between them. But that same winter, Edmund died, and the *witan* (general assembly) elected Canute as king (1016–35 CE). Canute accompanied his accession to the throne, which was legitimized following affirmation by the *witan*, with two acts: he married Ethelred's widow (Edmund's mother), who bore him a son, and he underwent Christian baptism. Carter and Mears describe how Canute's conversion to Christianity wrought a profound change in his behavior. He began to build monasteries, and saw to it that a Christian cleric, who had been cruelly killed by the Danes, was given his 'last rites' in the presence of the queen. Canute, in fact, was so liked by the Anglo-Saxons that he sent the Danish fleet and most of the Danish forces back to Denmark. From Denmark, he went on a campaign of conquest and conquered Norway; he thus became king of England, Denmark and Norway simultaneously.

Upon his death in 1035, his eldest son, Sweyn, inherited the Danish throne and England was divided into two kingdoms. One was given to his son Harold Harefoot, and the other to his son Harthacnut (his son by his second wife, Ethelred's widow, Emma of Normandy, who also had another son by her first husband). But Sweyn, the eldest son, died soon thereafter and Harthacnut went to Denmark to rule in his half-brother's place. For a time, he showed no interest in England until Harold was chosen (probably by the *witan* assembly, although Carter and Mears do not say so explicitly) to occupy the English throne. This choice prompted Harthacnut to invade England, in 1040, at the head of a Danish army, but when he arrived he found that his brother Harold had died. Thus Harthacnut, already king of both Denmark and Norway, also became king of England, but died two years later, in 1042, from the effects of strong drink. This brought to an end that stage of Danish rule in England. The *witan* now elected Edward (the dead king's half-brother, Emma's son from her first husband, Ethelred) as king. The Anglo-Saxon line once again ruled England, thanks to the fact that Emma had married the king of Denmark after the death of her first husband, the Anglo-Saxon king.

One of the Norman leaders was William, whose father (Prince Charles) was King Edward's cousin (Edward's mother Matilda was Charles's father's sister). Edward was childless and considered William to be a worthy successor. Godwin returned to the Thames with a war fleet, entered London, and convinced the *witan* assembly to return his title of earl of Wessex and to abolish the standing of the Norman nobles. Shortly thereafter, Godwin died; his son Harold became earl of Wessex. Harold was not long after captured by William when his ship went aground on a reef near the Normandy shore. As a prisoner, Harold was forced to swear fealty to William as the price for letting Harold go. When Edward died in 1066, the *witan* decided to install Harold on the throne; he accepted, thereby violating his oath of fealty to William, who thereupon prepared to invade England by sea and take the throne for himself, armed with a letter of appointment from the pope. In the ensuing battle, Harold was killed by William, who landed with his soldiers and cavalry (an innovation in England at the time) in southern England. William arrived in London and began negotiations with the *witan*, which decided to award him the throne (in the absence of any other candidate).

The Formation of Scotland

At the same time, Scotland experienced a number of events and vicissitudes of its own. Before the invasion of the Norsemen, Scotland was the home of four 'peoples' (to use Carter and Mears' terminology): Picts (in clusters in northern Scotland), Scots (in the northwest opposite the Irish coast from whence they came), Angles (along the eastern coast), and Britons (along the western coast). At this time, people of the same stock lived together according to their own traditions, undisturbed by other ethnic groups. When the Norsemen raided, however, the first two of the aforementioned groups came together. The Pict king and many of his knights were killed by the Norsemen following the Norse occupation of the island of Iona in the year 795. The king of the Scots, Kenneth, then became king of the Picts as well in 843.

The Norse invasion continued strongly against the Scottish people, conquering a great deal of Scottish land and causing the Scottish capital to be moved southwards, to Carlisle. By the tenth century CE, however, there were Norse defeats in battle against the English king Edward the Elder and his sons Athelstan and Edmund. The then-Scottish king, Malcolm, was unable to hold on to that remote area, whereupon Edmund did so instead, thereby becoming the Scottish king's chief lord there. The Scots continued to move northwards and, in the year 962, the son of the king of Scotland was able to take control of Edinburgh. During the rule of the Scottish King Malcolm II (1005–34 CE), the Scots gained control of northern Scotland and fortified the border between Scotland and England (at that point subject to the rule of Danish King Canute). By 1034 CE, all of Britain's northern regions were unified under the Scottish crown. The unification of Scotland is apparently due to the concerns that arose from about inheritance and threats from powerful external forces. Carter and Mears summarize the aforementioned events by saying that they united the five groups (Picts, Scots, Britons, Norsemen and English settlers in the Tweed region) into a single polity, which would subsequently require forging into a "single national entity" (in their words). Carter and Mears thus make an important distinction between the unification of groups from above by their rulers, and the unification from below by shared myths, fate, awareness and political will. Green has his own unique perspective on how the Anglo-Saxons evolved as a group during the period

1013–1204 CE, when Danish and other foreign kings ruled England. He states that the English, at this time, were transformed into a 'slave people' under foreign rule, which evolved into internal cohesion under Danish, Norman and Angevin kings.

The Normans

Feudalism, although already in existence in England, is often associated with the reign of William I (the conqueror). Feudalism determined the social structure of England from the Anglo-Saxon rule through the Danish raid up till the time of the Norman rule. The lands of England were held by feudal lords who subjugated and ruled over the affairs of villagers and nobles within the boundaries of their lands. A Norman lord had rule over affairs like marriage, vocation and so on. The lords ran a local court of justice which tried criminals and determined matters of inheritance.

William I

In his book, Green says that William I's authority derived from a double source: he was elected, and he had conquered England. By elected, he quite likely means that, according to English custom, when the king died, the throne devolved to his heir only after receiving the approval of a 'council of elders' representing the subjects, and therefore William I and his descendants, as conquerors, no longer needed this approval. Green further states that William II, the son and successor of William the Conqueror, defeated the barons who had rebelled against him by exploiting the hated of the English masses for the (Norman) barons; the masses seemed to him to be suffused with a spirit of English patriotism. Green thus apparently thought that the English masses (or at least the freemen) already possessed a spirit of English nationality as early as the end of the eleventh century CE.

The Crown and the Papacy

The then-pope supported William the Conqueror. When Pope Gregory VII's plan of subjugation of all kings to the papacy was known, William refused to pledge allegiance to the pope; he rejected the idea that all England was given to him (the king) by the pope as the supreme lord of kings. What ensued was a battle of wills between William and the pope in which William could be seen as the victor. In effect, bishops and clergymen of high office were chosen by English clerics and swore fealty to the king.

Henry II and Richard I

Geoffrey Plantagenet, the Count of Anjou, was Matilda's second husband and the father of Henry II, who was born eight years after the marriage of Matilda and the count. A year after his father's death, and shortly before he obtained the English throne, in 1152, Henry II married Eleanor, heiress of the duchy of Aquitaine in France. Before Henry II was crowned, there was a long battle between Henry's mother, Matilda (the daughter of Henry I), and Stephen (who had been crowned king of England). The end of this war saw King Stephen adopt Henry as his son and heir to the throne shortly before his death. Henry's marriage to Eleanor and title as English king saw him make claims three duchies in France, Normandy, and Anjou (the first of these duchies was his together with the English throne since it had belonged to his grandfather, Henry I, and the second he had inherited from his father, the Count of Anjou). These, together with his wife's duchy of Aquitaine, gave Henry control of over one-half of the territory of France.

Henry II was the first in a line of talented English kings. He left his impression on the English land and its laws – his deeds had a long-term effect on the English political system and contributed to the supremacy of the monarchy in England over the lords, the bishops and the other nobles of the realm. He is considered to be the father of the English system of justice and the father of the jury system, causing the people to put great trust in the justice meted out by the king's court. Therein laid the core of Henry's power: the fact that all crime and legislative power laid with the king. In this way, Henry strengthened the central government in England despite the feudal system. He ruled in such a manner that every Englishman sensed that the king was in full control of the land. The key to the king's authority lay in the Exchequer and the Royal Magistracy that exercised centralized control over the monarchy; the population became aware of the existence of a central government based on court functionaries and acting in the king's name. Justice throughout the kingdom was also administered by circuit judges, appointed in accordance with an act of the king in 1166.

In 1174, King Henry II passed away and his son Richard I succeeded him on the throne. Richard is recorded in history as a crusader and an ineffective ruler. He was only interested in amassing wealth from England, which he did by selling bishoprics, government posts and feudal magisterial rights to the highest bidders, as well as charters to London and other cities. In 1190, Richard I left on his crusade to the Holy Land, financed by the money that he had amassed. On his return journey in 1192, he was taken prisoner by Leopold, Duke of Austria, for having previously insulted the latter. Leopold was paid a ransom, collected by means of a land tax equal to one-quarter of the total income from the assets of Richard's English subjects. After his release, Richard went to England for a short visit. The rest of his life was spent in wars in France against his companion on the Crusade, the king of France, who had attempted to take over Normandy in Richard's absence. Richard died in 1199.

Kings John and Henry III

King John was an untrustworthy person who quarreled with powerful adversaries, had a bad character and was a poor monarch. He quarreled with his nephew Arthur, duke of Brittany, as well as with a nobleman from Aquitaine whose fiancée he married after divorcing his own wife, who came from an aristocratic English family. Philip, king of France, with the help of Arthur of Brittany, invaded the duchy of Normandy which John had inherited. John had made himself numerous enemies, including Arthur, whom he later captured and had killed. John was also involved in yet another quarrel, this time with the pope, after Walter, the archbishop of Canterbury, died. What transpired was the monks wanted to install a successor to the archbishop (without consulting either the king or the bishops), and sent the chosen archbishop to Rome in order to receive the pope's blessing. The bishops, infuriated at this event, sent an appeal against the election to the pope, while the king decided to appoint a candidate of his own choice. The pope, on hearing all sides in this dispute, appointed another person entirely, the English Cardinal Stephen Langton, whom he dispatched to England. King John was furious and prevented the cardinal from entering English territory. Pope Innocent III's response was to place a papal ban on all of England. John, in alliance with the Holy Roman Emperor Otto IV, also wanted to subjugate France but was defeated, while Otto IV lost his throne to Frederick II. Upon his return in defeat from France, John found both the Church and the nobility united against him. Even the cities supported the rebels, led by Archbishop Langton, whose power base lay in the barons' united army. John had no choice but to accede to the rebels' demands. This concession, in 1215, took the form of a document: the Magna Carta. The king, in 1216 CE, lost the royal treasury, fell ill and died.

Henry III succeeded King John at the age of nine. Two people, however, ruled in his name at this time: William Marshall, earl of Pembroke, and the judge Hubert de Burgh. The two aforementioned men ruled the land; two years later, the earl died and the judge continued to rule alone until Henry III's maturity. At maturity, Henry III took over the throne and imprisoned the judge, and ruled with the help of his teacher, Peter des Roches, who was appointed bishop of Winchester. Henry III was England's crowned monarch in the years 1234–72 CE, but he proved insufficiently able to rule over such a turbulent country as England was in those days. Due to his poor rule, a coalition of barons appointed a committee of twenty-four barons, whose authority was similar to that of an elected parliament and which became known as the 'Oxford Parliament'. In 1258, the committee published the 'Oxford Provisions' as a basis for the administration of the kingdom. Two members of the committee were appointed as a permanent council to oversee the activities of the king's government. These two members were the earl de Monfort and the earl de Clave. Thus, for a time, England was ruled by a type of oligarchy. Henry III took an oath to obey the Provisions but, a year later,

Pope Alexander IV released him from this oath. Both parties agreed to bring the matter before the king of France, who decided in favor of the king. The coalition, however, refused to accept this decision and its troops defeated the army of the king, took both the king and his son Edward prisoner, and installed the earl de Montfort as the head of the government. Henry subsequently died in 1272.

In the period presently under discussion, England experienced turbulent times that affected not only the nobility and clergy, but also many commoners and burghers from the towns. These events influenced broad classes of the English populace; the urban population began to take an active part in these events, which provided the basis and background for many myths that shaped the English character, and gave rise to a distinction between those whose lives were centered in England (even if they were Norman by origin) and those whose stay in the country was temporary. *This is how a relatively broad sector of the English public began to possess a national identity. The myths did not correspond with the historical facts, but they created an awareness which grew into a foundation for the uniquely English social structure.*

Edward I, Edward II, Wales and Scotland

Edward I

Edward I, unlike his father before, was a more efficient king by comparison who never made the same mistake twice. His experience was due to his previous administration of large estates in Gascony (France), Wales and Ireland, as well as in England. His rule was anything but despotic and cruel. He did his best to involve all elements – barons, knights, the clergy and the cities – in political decision-making.

Edward was known to favor advice from professional administrators and legal experts rather than the great barons. Edward I was also known to have engineered the expulsion of the kingdom's Jews in 1290. Carter and Mears point out that the number of Jews (and their influence) had grown in England since the Norman conquest. Immediately upon his accession to the throne, Edward I decreed a ban on usury and expelled all the Jews from his kingdom. During his reign, Edward I enforced a number of laws that were instrumental in the development of England as a nation. He further centralized the crown and helped improve the economy with various laws. Edward I's statutes were presented and approved at sessions of the Great Council; a number of full parliaments also met during his reign. In the thirteenth century CE, the king was the most important figure in the parliaments that he convened, heading a membership that consisted of barons, commoners, clergymen and representatives of the urban communities (from whence derives the parliamentary term 'commons'). The parliament that Edward I convened in 1295 is considered to be the model for all future parliaments, exemplified by Edward I's declaration that "What touches all should be approved by all." *In this light, it is important to draw attention to a significant matter concerning Edward I's standing among the English. Green states that Edward I saw himself as a 'national English' king, as did his subjects who no longer considered him a foreigner as they had his forefathers. Thus, with Edward I, the age of foreign kings came to an end.*

A Brief Historical Overview of Wales

The Anglo-Saxon word *wales* means 'land of foreigners'. The Welsh call their land *cymry* – 'land of friends'. After the collapse of Roman rule in Britain, the Welsh were in control of the entire western part of Britain from Cumberland to Cornwall. For a time, neighboring English kingdoms encroached upon this territory, but there then ensued a period of some three hundred years during which these trespasses ceased. Due to the nature of their natural terrain, the Welsh were ruled by a number of Welsh princes who warred against each other. Welsh society was divided into clans based upon ancestral bloodlines, similar to the Scottish family groups. After the Norman conquest, William established three earldoms along the Welsh border from which attacks into Wales were conducted. During the reign of the English king Rufus, most of southern and central Wales came under Norman rule. The Norman barons were notorious for their cruelty even in that barbaric age, causing the Welsh efforts to eject them, which were later successful in the northern and central parts of Wales. The political instability during King Stephen's reign provided the Welsh with the opportunity to expand their territory, and even Henry II did not succeed in preventing the unification of Wales under Rhys ap Gruffydd, known as Lord Rhys. When Lord Rhys died in 1197, there was no viable successor except for Llywelyn ap Lorwerth, prince of Gwynedd – an important figure during his rule (1194–1240 CE). In 1218, he signed an agreement with the English king Henry III whereby he turned three fortresses over to the English monarch. Llywelyn, known as 'the Great', was now master of a unified Wales. After Llywelyn died in 1240, Wales experienced a period of disruption and decline. In 1254, Henry III appointed his son Edward lord over the Welsh areas seized by the English. Llywelyn the Great's grandson, Llywelyn ap Gruffydd, at first ruled over those territories unconquered by England, but later expanded his domains at the expense of the English, particularly in southern Wales. In 1267, England recognized his conquests and acknowledged him as the prince of Wales. Llywelyn, however, failed to recognize Edward I as his lord, whereby Edward seized Llywelyn's fiancée, Eleanor (Elinor in Welsh), daughter of Simon de Montfort, and imprisoned her. Edward's adversity caused the princes of southern Wales withdrew their allegiance to Llywelyn in 1276 CE, whose territory was now reduced to his original holdings (Gwynedd).

Edward II

Edward II (1307–27 CE) was unable to conquer Scotland, therefore had to recognize Scottish independence in 1311. At the beginning of his reign, the king took a childhood friend, named Gaveston, as his closest advisor. This rankled with the barons, who rebelled against this decision, going as far to assassinate Gaveston and even start a rebellion against the king. The king, however, ended the rebellion and caught and executed the conspirators in 1322. The king, after this, was made to appear before the Parliament where it was decided that the king would have to submit his political initiatives for parliamentary approval. By implication, the Commons had greater supremacy than the barons had over the king, which meant that the king could not act freely in his capacity as ruler. Edward II then requested his wife to hold diplomatic discussions with her brother, the king of France. The queen, however, moved from France to Flanders accompanied by her lover, Baron Mortimer. These two plotters landed with a military force, seized power in England, then caught and imprisoned the king. Later, the king was murdered, but not before he agreed to abdicate the throne in favor of his son, Edward III, who was thirteen years of age at the time. After Edward III acceded to the throne, political power remained in the hands of his mother and Baron Mortimer at first but, by the time Edward III was seventeen years old, the king had Mortimer arrested, tried for treason and executed. The king's mother retired from politics. In all this time, Parliament received notice of all these events and approved them retroactively, showing how important the position of Parliament in England had become. This unprecedented request by the monarch in seeking the approval of Parliament (and informing it of victories) became a tradition which has been maintained ever since. Carter and Mears note that the events above marked the beginning of another tradition – that of murder – which would accompany the English monarchy for generations. This unnatural custom naturally affected both English history and the English people's attitude to their monarchy. It was a motivation around which grew the memories and myths that built the English collective consciousness.

Edward III

In 1327, Edward III became king of England, under the circumstances described above. His reign is perhaps most notable for the wars he fought. Only three years into his reign, he sent an army to support the side of Edward Balliol, titular king of the Scots, in the civil war raging in Scotland. He then waged a war against the French king because of his support for the Scottish king, David II, who had found refuge in the French court. Edward III concluded that his war in Scotland would not have a successful outcome while France continued to support David II against Edward Balliol. When Edward III left Scotland, David II returned and defeated Edward Balliol.

When the French King Charles IV died without male issue or brothers in 1328, Edward III made a claim to the throne from his mother's side; however, the French chose to give the throne to Philip VI, the deceased king's nephew (his brother's son). Edward III also waged a war against Flanders, because of his quarrel with the prince of Flanders who, in turn, forbade his country from trading with England. This trade was important to England as the flourishing Flemish cloth industry was the best customer for the wool produced by English sheep. When war broke out, in 1338, between France and England, the Flemish, led by the merchant James van Artevelde, agreed to act in concert with Edward III; the prince of Flanders was forced to flee to France. It was from this period, until the reign of George III, that the kings of England also entitled themselves king of France, on the strength of that claim to the French throne. George III formally (and finally) renounced the title in 1801. The conflict with France eventually became known as the French 'Hundred Years' War'.

Another thing Edward III's reign is noted for is the steps he took to strengthen commerce and manufacturing in England. In the fourteenth century CE, England was the main source of wool for the continent, and a major exporter of hides and tin. The king imposed high taxes on exports, and his income grew. The garment industry was greatly promoted and support was afforded the traditional dominant guilds in various artificial ways. Within a century, the domestic textile industry had helped to make England a rich country. The legislation put forward by both the king and Parliament insisted on protecting English interests, even at the cost of the external relations fostered by the king. This was a case not only of Parliament following the king's lead, but also of the king following Parliament's. The English Parliament thus became independent from the king in legislation and policy. *This was a part of the process broadening the circle of political participation in English society; a process described with careful attention in the course of the present work in order to illuminate and explain the social development that led to the maturation of the English national identity.* The English language and its literature matured during Edward III's reign. Previously, the language spoken at court was French, and the common people spoke various distinct dialects. In the second half of the thirteenth century CE, England's upper classes began to speak English.

Richard II and Lancaster

John of Gaunt, Edward III's son, and the transition to Richard II

After Edward the Black Prince ceased his activities in France, his younger brother, John of Gaunt, duke of Lancaster (who had married the heiress of the House of Lancaster), became the dominant figure at court. John was also given a free hand, in the year 1371, to appoint ministers as he saw fit. During the five years of his rule, the ministers whom he appointed amassed wealth dishonestly at the expense of the public treasury. In 1377, Edward III died and, because the Black Prince had predeceased him, he was succeeded by his grandson Richard II, the son of the Black Prince. The new king was ten years old and his mother ruled in his name. A new cabinet, made up of people who had been friends of the king's mother, replaced John and his ministers. There was popular discontent within England at the wealth of the Church and its subordination to popes of French origin. This criticism was also leveled by John (the king's uncle who had ruled the country in the name of King Richard II's grandfather) and John Wycliffe, a former minister appointed by John and later dismissed by the mother of the new king. Because of the criticism of the Church's wealth, the English Parliament proposed that grants to the Church be prohibited and that land which had been granted to the Church be returned. Wycliffe played a leading role in this debate. He had studied at Oxford and remained there to teach. He claimed that the clergy in England had taken positions which were more suited to secular people.

In his later years, King Richard II became a despot and was revolted against by the British peasants, the barons and the Parliament. What ensued was that he was forced to abdicate after being captured by Henry, the son of his elder uncle the duke of Lancaster, after the duke died, and Richard expropriated most of his uncle's lands, thereby violating the inheritance rights of Henry (the king's cousin). Henry was approached by numerous barons who had been shocked by the king's actions – this was a step which meant that any baron in England might be liable to forfeit his estate to the king upon his death instead of being able to bequeath it to his eldest son as was the custom. Henry arrived in Britain and was joined by numerous barons, including the earl of Northumberland – the owner of the largest estate in northern England. Richard II was forced to sign a letter of abdication. According to accepted practice, the throne should now have gone to another member of the royal family, but Henry decided that he wanted to be crowned as King Henry IV. He convened Parliament, read Richard II's abdication document, and announced his claim to the throne. Parliament reacted with cries of support. One year later, the former king was murdered in his cell on the orders of the king-elect. This was the first time that a king had been elected by Parliament, contradicting the principle of the inheritance of the crown by the grace of God. Parliament had now replaced God. It had become possible for the king of England to rule 'by the grace of Parliament'. Parliament's role as an elector of the king enhanced its status.

Henry IV (1399–1413 CE)

The first-half of Henry IV's reign was beset with continuous rebellions due to the nature of his ascension. The uprisings were mostly led by barons who adopted the king's own example: they rebelled because they wanted to improve their own situation by force. In Wales, another motive was the general desire on the part of the Welsh populace to rid itself of its English overlords. Henry IV used military force to put down the rebellions. He captured the rebel leaders and had them executed after a summary trial in which they were not given the opportunity to defend themselves and no real evidence was presented. Parliament had gained the authority to raise taxes and to choose the king and, without its help, Henry IV would not have been able to resist those who rebelled against him. Since the king was dependent on Parliament, the latter forced the king to agree to consult with a commission appointed by Parliament and subject to parliamentary supervision. In the last five years of Henry's reign, he suffered from serious health problems and was incapable of executing his duties properly. The supervisory commission was split into two rival parties: one headed by the prince of Wales (later Henry V) and the other by the Archbishop Arundel. At his death, Henry V ascended the throne of England.

Henry V (1413–1422 CE)

The first challenge to the new king, Henry V, was the religious sect of the Lollards. These were Christians who did not recognize the authority of the pope, whom they called the 'anti-Christ'. The Church in England considered them heretics and, in 1401, Parliament enacted a special law concerning the Lollards and authorizing them to be burnt at the stake. One of them had already been burnt at the stake before the law was passed; now others saved their lives by recanting. Henry pursued the campaign against the Lollards with great vigor and cruelty.

The Conquest of France

Henry V strove to enhance his legitimacy in England. He did this by waging war in France on the pretext of the English kings' claim to the French throne, based firstly upon his right of inheritance and secondly upon his marriage to Isabella, the daughter of the French king and crown princess. Henry V landed in France, in the summer of 1415, with twenty thousand troops. In the course of a siege of a French city, two-thirds of the English soldiers died of dysentery, but the English continued to advance and defeated a heavily-armored French army thanks to the superior mobility of their forces. Henry V was victorious in battle against an army four-times as large as his own: this was the Battle of Agincourt that took place on 25 October 1415; five thousand French soldiers were killed along with hundreds of Englishmen, including the duke of York. After Agincourt, the English began to conquer Normandy; they besieged one city after another, while the French government remained paralyzed by the internal struggles between the two parties – those of the dukes of Burgundy and Orleans. During his lifetime, Henry V demonstrated considerable courage; he was a good, capable leader, but wasted his country's resources on wars in foreign lands.

The Middle Ages

In the fifteenth century CE, England and Europe experienced great changes, reflected in England by the Peasants' Revolt and Wycliffe's attacks on the Church. Other changes included the gradual abolition of serfdom and the emergence of a commercial class. Wycliffe's actions foreshadowed the Reformation movement in Germany led by Luther (born in 1483 CE) against the Church. The Wars of the Roses affected the long history of the British by bringing about an end to the influence of the barons, thus opening the way to the growth of the power of Parliament.

CHAPTER TWO

The Renaissance

Carter and Mears define the Renaissance as a change which affected Europe in the period between the fourteenth and the sixteenth centuries CE, in the wake of a continental revival of ancient Greek art, literature and science. This change affected every facet of life in Europe. The main cause of this development, they assert, was a basic shift in attitude: a transition from obedience of authority (with suffering as a virtue) to a view that encouraged men to seek their own answers to life's questions – and attached a greater importance to life's pleasures. *The spirit of the Renaissance gave rise to the concepts of nation, nationality and the supremacy of the state. It also contributed to the separation of Church and state, varying by degree in the different European countries.* Before the Renaissance, the Latin language that was used throughout the continent expressed the Christian world's unity and uniformity despite the different vernaculars used by the various groups. In matters religious and political, Latin helped the educated classes throughout Europe to feel that they belonged to a single collective Christian society. Europe's various peoples were all subjects of Christendom, headed by the pope and the emperor. *But from the Renaissance, the idea of national allegiance gradually emerged and Europe no longer seemed united. The groups that assumed leadership roles in Europe were those that had attained internal national unity – in France, Spain and England. Italy remained divided into city-states; Germany also failed to unite.* Renaissance teachings reached England during the reigns of Edward IV, Henry VII and Henry VIII.

The New Kingdoms (Henry VII and the start of Henry VIII's reign)

By the time the Tudor King Henry VII ascended the throne in 1485, the English had already been a single national entity for quite some time. But political authority was not unified due to the power of the feudal barons, and the Tudor kings were forced to put their kingdom in order. When they acted to impose their political authority on the barons and the Church, they were able to do so because they were wise enough to make use of Parliament in order to maintain contact with the people at large. Henry VII's reign was rocky at first, with different plans to overthrow him, but eventually his reign stabilized. He made policies that enhanced the economic and commercial power of England.

His son, Henry VIII, took over after his death. He was a young and aggressive king. Henry VIII introduced the Protestant Reformation into England. It was not an act of faith but of political expediency. He wanted to divorce his wife, Catherine, because she could not bear him a son, but divorce was not allowed in the Catholic Church. So he introduced the Protestant Reformation into England so he could marry another wife. This caused a rift between him and the Roman Empire. Henry VIII severed his ties to the papacy and turned England into a Catholic country without a pope. During the reign of Edward VI, England rushed into Protestantism; an English-language prayer book was adopted, churches were destroyed and ancient rituals were abandoned.

Henry VIII received a good education. No one expected this young, handsome, athletic monarch (who became king at the age of eighteen) to act as aggressively as he did. During the first twenty years of his reign (1509–29 CE), when Thomas Wolsey was the dominant figure in the cabinet, Henry VIII focused mainly on foreign affairs. Henry allied with Pope Julius II and Spain against France, and won an easy victory in its first battle. Henry VIII placed the English army in France under the command of Wolsey, a man of humble origins who had graduated from university at the age of fifteen and had embarked on a clerical and political career. In his later years, Henry VIII broke with the papacy and introduced a new system (similar to the Reformation changes) into England. Henry VIII introduced the Protestant Reformation into England as an act not of faith, but of political expediency. The conflict between Henry VIII and the pope concerned the king's marital problems; he was responsible for withdrawing the English nation from under the Roman-Catholic umbrella of the papacy. The matter arose after Henry and Catherine had been married for eighteen years, during which Catherine gave birth seven times, but all the newborn infants died – with the exception of their daughter, Mary. Following the deaths of his sons, King Henry VIII believed that God might be punishing him for his marriage to Catherine, who had also been married to his late brother. Wolsey used this opportunity to play on the king's fears, and urged the king to ask the pope to declare his marriage to Catherine null and void; in this way, relations between England and Spain would deteriorate and Wolsey would be able to promote his favored policy of an alliance with France. The pope was reluctant to make a clear assent to Henry VIII's request so as to avoid difficulties in his relations with the Spanish king (who was also Holy Roman Emperor), so he decided to appoint Wolsey and another cardinal to resolve the issue. Unable to come to an agreement, the two broke off their deliberations in order to seek papal advice on the matter. The result was that Wolsey no longer enjoyed the king's royal favor, where he was first stripped of his titles and sent to the Tower, where he contracted dysentery, was taken to the abbey of Leicester and died. According to Green, this paved the way for Henry VIII's absolute rule over England, because the only power in England which had been able to control him to some extent – the Church – became powerless after Wolsey's death.

With this step, coupled with the appointment of a clergyman by the name of Thomas Cranmer (a relative of Anne Boleyn), Henry invalidated his marriage to Catherine, married Anne at a secret ceremony and appointed Cranmer as archbishop of Canterbury, who convened an ecclesiastical court which declared the king's marriage to Catherine void and made the fact of the marriage to Anne public a month later. Anne gave birth to a daughter, Elizabeth, who would one day become queen.

The pope, in response, named the newborn girl illegitimate and excommunicated Henry VIII. The king, however, took further steps: namely, passing additional legislation stating that only candidates proposed by the king would be appointed as bishops, the English throne would be inherited by Queen Anne's descendants, and that all public servants were required to pledge their allegiance to the king and to declare that the king's authority in ecclesiastical matters was superior to that of the pope. Anyone who refused to make this pledge (Thomas More and the bishop of Rochester were among those who refused) would be sentenced to death. Green states – after More's death – the old English liberties happened to become meaningless. The king's proclamations took the place of laws of Parliament, and the crown's will replaced due process. In the religious sphere, the concept of 'His Majesty' replaced that of divine sanctity. The clergy at all levels, from the archbishop down to the simplest priest, sounded like echoes of the royal will. Only the king was authorized to determine what was true, and what heresy was.

Edward VI was a weak and much-loved child. His father's strong hand had succeeded in coping with the struggle between Catholics and Protestants during the final decade of his reign. Henry VIII appointed a council of ministers to help his small son, headed by the king's uncle, the Protestant Edward Seymour (an earl who became duke of Somerset, henceforth: Somerset), who was appointed by the council of ministers as 'Defender of the King' from the years 1547–49 CE. Somerset's first concern was Scotland. In keeping with Henry VIII's idea, he tried to promote King Edward VI's marriage to Mary Queen of Scots. When persuasion proved futile, he invaded Scotland and, in 1547, defeated the Scots. Hereafter, the hearsay laws were abolished, including the punishment of burning at the stake. This led to the advent of a wave of protestant from various nations introducing new doctrines.

Edward VI was in poor health (he died at the age of fifteen). Before his death, Northumberland persuaded him to sign a will naming as his heir Jane, granddaughter of his aunt Mary who, according to Henry VIII's will, stood in line of succession only after Edward VI's sisters, Mary and Elizabeth. Northumberland's obvious motive was that Jane was his own daughter-in-law and, with her on the throne, he could continue to rule England. Edward VI died shortly after signing his will, and Northumberland immediately arranged for Jane's coronation. However, he was forced to leave hastily at the head of an army in order to confront the troops of Mary, Edward VI's sister, who had departed to England's eastern counties where Northumberland was particularly hated. At the same time, the Privy Council met and declared Edward

VI's will null and void, reaffirming Henry VIII's will according to which the throne now belonged to Mary, Henry VIII's eldest daughter. Northumberland realized that the game was up, and surrendered. Mary I, queen of England, entered a jubilant London – for whose residents the fact that Mary would be England's next queen was glad news indeed.

Queen Mary I

When Queen Mary I became queen, she burnt Protestants at the stake; some three hundred men and women were burnt at the stake throughout England during the course of the persecution of Protestants during Mary I's reign. *Burning at the stake has accompanied the English over generations as a myth of collective grandeur of the type which builds a national identity. Such myths can steel a collective to withstand great hardships and help to create cohesive groups reinforced with a stiff moral backbone. This is what gives today's Britons a unique strength which is lacking in most other contemporary European groups.*

Elizabeth I ascended the throne in 1558, at the age of twenty-five. The English would undergo a fourth phase in the vicissitudes of religious policy during the reign of Elizabeth. During Elizabeth I's reign (1558–1603 CE), the English enjoyed two supreme achievements. One was material and the other spiritual: the geographical discoveries made by English seamen, and the wealth of literature produced by English poets and dramatists. The reign of this skilled and capable monarch was also characterized by her successful political efforts to maneuver around numerous dangers and obstacles with the help of her hand-picked and talented ministers. She succeeded in maintaining English independence in both religious and political spheres.

Reformation

Protestant movements were born as a result of the actions and ways of life practiced by the Catholic papacy in the late fifteenth century. The Protestantism was championed by various parties in Europe who felt there was a need for change to the old ways. Chief among them was the monk Martin Luther who, on his journey through Europe, noticed the corrupt practices of the high-ranking Catholic Church officials and made no pains to speak against them. There were also Savonarola and Colet, amongst others. Luther's aim was to show the depravity of the papacy and the Roman Catholic Church as a whole; he translated the bible into German and spoke against the papacy. The Church, in response, declared him to be a heretic and excommunicated him for these actions. In the course of this rebellion, some German princes supported Luther and gave him their protection while others sided with the church, whereby a conflict arose between both parties. The English king (Henry VIII), on his part, rebutted him and was, because of this action, conferred the title 'Defender of the Faith' by the pope; this title is still held by the English monarchy till this day. After the war had calmed, a new principle swept across Europe and Protestantism was born.

Queen Elizabeth I's Policies

Faced with the religious upheaval left to her by the two previous reigns (Catholicism on the part of Mary and Protestantism during Edward VI's reign), Elizabeth was charged with the task of finding a balance in the way of political reform in the Church. Elizabeth had two pressing problems at the start of her reign: the fact that some segments of society (predominantly Catholics) did not accept her as her father's heir (as a result of the circumstances that led to her birth) and the imminent invasion threat posed by the Spanish Armada.

As regards the first problem, the key issue was the plot to assassinate Elizabeth and replace her with Queen Mary of Scotland on the throne. At the time, Mary had been recently ousted from Scotland by the nobles and citizens, where she had been forced to abdicate in favor of her son James because of her actions, which made the Scots feel that their queen was immoral and unfit to rule. *The actions of the nobles in consortium with the people can be said to have constituted a step towards uniting the Scots into a single entity – a step towards the creation of a national identity.*

The captured Queen Mary was later able to escape and seek asylum with Queen Elizabeth I in England. This event led to the aforementioned plot against Elizabeth, which was set in motion by the Catholics in consort with the Spanish King Philip II. The conspirators wanted to replace Elizabeth – a Protestant – with Mary, a Catholic. A rebellion was started, but did not receive anticipated support from Philip II and was disbanded, with the ringleaders caught, sentenced and executed. With the plot exposed, Mary Queen of Scots was put on trial, found guilty and also executed subsequently – although this was not approved by Elizabeth.

The second problem (the threat of the Spanish Armada) was solved by Elizabeth through the use of covert plots that weakened the Spanish fleet. Elizabeth I sponsored privateers who continually attacked the Spanish on the sea. Philip II declared war against the English in 1585. By 1588, the Armada was defeated by English heavy gun-ships developed during the time of Henry VIII. The gun-ships were able to fire at the Spanish fleet at long range and then retreat. At the end of the war in 1604, the English had gained superiority over the seas.

CHAPTER THREE

The Long Eighteenth Century (1688–1815 CE)

Eighteenth-century Britain was an era of routine. This was the period before the advent of railroads, steam engines and other mechanical tools; a period when Britain enjoyed political stability. In this era, as a result of the 1688 constitutional reform, the gentry held the powers of rule. By now, the governing principle was thus: 'Parliament is supreme, and the aristocracy controlled Parliament'; this replaced the earlier principle of the king ruling 'by the grace of God'. In the later course of this period (during the reign of George III), Britain found itself in a confrontation with its American colonies; eventually, in 1783, Britain recognized their independence. There were also struggles and wars with other imperial powers where Britain notably successful. Military and naval traditions came into being, engendered by such prominent leaders as Nelson, Rodney, Wolfe and Clive. Britain seized the Cape Colony in South Africa from the Dutch (in 1806 CE), occupied India (in the years 1575–1805 CE), and began to colonize Australia (from 1788 CE).

William and Mary and the Changes under Queen Anne

The Convention Parliament of 1689 proclaimed the supremacy of Parliament, and imposed the following four restrictions on the monarch's authority:

- The king may not suspend laws passed by Parliament.
- The king may not levy taxes without parliamentary consent.
- The king may not maintain an army in peacetime without parliamentary consent.
- The king may not interfere in parliamentary elections; Parliament is free to deliberate any topic, and may convene as often as it likes; the king may not be a Catholic, nor may he marry one; religious toleration would be maintained, but no Catholics may serve in His Majesty's Government.

William III, the king at this time, was an unpopular king. His main goal was to weaken Louis XIV; to this, he dedicated the first eight years of his rule in England. William III formed his own cabinet (composed of members of the Whig party), headed the cabinet and dealt personally with foreign affairs, although he had no choice but to work together with Parliament. Parliament later passed an Act which determined the succession to the English Crown; the Act gave succession rights to Mary's sister, Anne, if William and Mary died childless. If Anne too died childless, the throne would pass to James I's granddaughter, the electress of Hanover (in Germany) and her descendants – which is indeed what happened. The electress died in the year in which the Act was passed (1700 CE), and so, after William III's death, the throne of England (and Britain) passed to George, son of the electress, later George I of England.

Similarly, the Scottish held a Convention in 1689 which was similar to the Parliament, but it was not convened by the king. The Convention also passed an act of succession in line with the Act passed in England. Scotland, at the time, was plagued with internal struggles which William and Mary helped to settle, thereby gaining acceptance from the Scots. At this time, the Scots were afforded the opportunity to manage their own religious affairs without external intervention. As a result, the Scots proclaimed the Presbyterian Church to be the Church of Scotland; for the first time, Scotland had a 'national' church of its own. The Scottish Parliament was now free to make decisions for the first time since 1603 – its independence lasted for eighteen years. The English and Scottish Parliaments passed an Act of Union in 1707. This Act abolished the Scottish Parliament and installed Scottish peers and members of Parliament into the English House of Lords and House of Commons. Such was the culmination of Queen Elizabeth I's wise policy, which neutralized the bitter feelings of the Scots towards the English. Instead of the two separate political entities of England and Scotland, a single unit named Britain now came into existence; Wales had been unified with England long before. Britain thus became a single polity, with the exception of Ireland.

The Irish, on the other hand, did not consider the revolution of 1688 as 'glorious'. The Catholic Irish supported the Catholic James II, who landed in Ireland with a French army, in 1689, in his campaign to obtain the English throne. James II was conquered in 1690 by William III. The English eventually captured the last Catholic bastion, which surrendered on the condition that the Catholics in Ireland would retain their properties and freedom of worship. The English Parliament also passed another legislation against non-Anglican Protestants (which included the vast majority of Irish Protestants); both situations saw to it that the Irish as a whole suffered oppression at the hands of the English. These were blows in addition to the legislation passed in the reign of Charles II, which had had a deleterious effect on the livestock trade in Ireland; Ireland thus became a 'backyard' for Britain, which now encompassed the entire British Isles, including Scotland, Wales and Ireland. Britain was now more united than it had been before the Glorious Revolution.

William III and Louis XIV

William, along with the alliance which included the Spanish, the Dutch and the Germans, fought the so-called 'Augsburg League War', lasting from 1689 to 1697, against Louis XIV. The English had a strategic interest in preventing the (Protestant) Low Countries from falling into foreign hands. The guiding principle of all governments – and the English-British government specifically – was that future generations would help the present generation to finance the current war; therefore, a company whose purpose was to lend money to the government was established in England (which had become Britain); this company, founded through liberal initiative, would become the Bank of England. The Augsburg War ended in a stalemate of sorts. It saw the Spanish crown fall into the hands of the same dynasty that ruled France. Louis XIV, at the other end, agreed to the presence of Dutch garrisons on the French and Belgian borders and recognized the existing regime in England while, in North America, an exchange of territories took place between England (Britain) and France. William III died in 1702 CE, in a fall from a horse; since he had no heirs, the throne devolved to Anne, sister of his late wife.

Queen Anne and Marlborough

The War of the Spanish Succession was fought in four different regions: Europe, America, the Atlantic Ocean and the Mediterranean Sea. In Europe, the war was waged variously in the Low Countries, Germany, Italy, Portugal and Catalonia. The English under Marlborough surprised the renowned French army in Germany, by attacking from a marshy and supposedly impassable area; they captured the French commander and killed and captured a great number of French soldiers, while suffering only light casualties themselves. Later the English, together with their allies in Germany, succeeded in wresting Belgium from Spanish control; the English navy captured Gibraltar and the island of Minorca in the Balearics. In 1706, British troops landed near Barcelona and the Catalans assisted them by rebelling against King Philip V of Spain. The English also advanced from Portugal in cooperation with the Portuguese, whom they enticed to side with them by signing a commercial treaty giving Portuguese wines preference on the British market over wines from France. But, in the same year, the French army moved into Spain to support Philip V, reducing British control in the area to just Catalonia and Gibraltar.

By 1710 CE (when the various fronts were at an impasse and the English public felt alienated from the government because of perceived violations of religious principles), the Queen Anne was convinced to replace the Whig cabinet with a Tory one, and to dismiss Marlborough from his command. Immediately after forming a government, the Tories called for parliamentary elections, in which they won a majority. This was as a result of the increased participation of educated Britons in national politics. This socio-political development was of immense importance to the internal development of Britain. The English ended their military operations on their own initiative, even before the Treaty of Utrecht was formally signed in 1713. From this treaty, Britain emerged as a European power of the first rank. The English also succeeded in reducing the danger posed by Louis XIV, but failed to bring about an annulment of the French-Spanish alliance.

The Whig Rule

Due to the failing health of Queen Anne, the Whigs initiated contact with the elector of Hanover, George Louis. The queen passed away on 1 August 1714, and the Whigs, together with the new prime minister, invited the elector of Hanover (whose mother had died previously) to assume the English-British crown – which he accepted and was later crowned as George I at the age of fifty-four. George I's first steps as king were to dismiss the Tory prime minister and to appoint a cabinet consisting of Whigs only, understanding that most Tories were loyal to James III (the pretender to the English throne) and not to him. George I did not speak English well; he allowed the Whigs to rule the country in his name (as also did his son and successor, George II). Whigs held the key positions in the church, in the army and in the fleet, and the country's judges knew that their chances for advancement depended upon Whig politicians, who thus ruled supreme everywhere – until the accession of George III to the throne.

In 1721, however, the government fell due to the failure of the South Sea Company to which the government had granted a monopoly on trade. The government was thus blamed for the losses to the company's shareholders, and the prime minister was replaced. A career-politician, Sir Robert Walpole, was chosen as prime minister. He is generally regarded as the first prime minister of Britain (the term was not in use at that time). This is significant, as it shows how public opinion of the time affected political action – the king could not afford to ignore the opinion of his subjects. *England, in this respect, had attained a level of development conducive to broad social involvement in politically- and economically-significant decision-making. Such development is a sign of progress in social cohesion, which forms the basis for the emergence of a national identity.*

The Industrial Revolution

Wesley represented an aspect of the division of Britain into two worlds which existed side-by-side:
- Those with plenty to eat, who lived a life of luxury, consumed culture and held political power through their representatives in Parliament.
- The hungry, relegated to the margins of political power, who adhered to a spiritual-religious vision; some were exiled and helped populate the New World, while others added an ethical dimension to their own society. They had, as yet, no political power or representation in either the Whig party or in Parliament, and did not influence legislation.

This description of the cleavage of British society is related to the Industrial Revolution, which enriched those in Britain who possessed capital and improved the political standing of Britain to the detriment of many in the British lower classes.

In the eighteenth century CE, Parliament passed specific Acts to enclose agricultural land in certain areas of the countryside. Nearly every Act was passed with the support of the estate owners, whose representatives sat in Parliament. The many that lost their land due to this legislation were forced to move from their native villages to join the class of industrial workers in the cities. As a result, the urban population of Britain increased from about one-fifth (in 1696 CE) to one-half (in 1769 CE) of the total population; subsequently, it continued to rise. Carter and Mears state that, between 1750 and 1850, Britain was transformed from an agricultural into an industrial society, and that the main causes of this transformation were the Enclosure Acts described above. Agriculture was now based on large estates, which were more efficient and economically viable compared with the old system of small individual farms and common village land worked collectively by the villagers. It thus appears that Britain's transformation into an industrial state owes more to the expulsion of farmers from their lands (a negative development) than to those farmers being attracted to the cities (a positive development). This process was unique to Britain; it brought about an enhancement of the status of the British Parliament – an institution which was also unique in Europe.

Ireland (1775–1800 CE)

During the last quarter of the eighteenth century CE, the Irish suffered repression at the hands of their English overlords. The Catholic landowners lost their estates – appropriated by English and Scottish Protestants. Only Protestants had the right to vote, but Ireland's own Protestants were Presbyterians and, as members of the Irish Parliament, they were forbidden to enact laws which had not been previously passed by an Act of Parliament in London. This state of affairs aroused the Irish to take steps to promote their rights; their leader was an Irish Protestant patriot and a skilled orator named Henry Grattan. Grattan was able, through good standing and the external threat of a French invasion of Ireland, to advocate a policy where some of the restrictions imposed on Ireland by England were eased. Grattan, therefore, headed the Irish government between 1783 and 1793, while Pitt remained the British prime minister.

Subsequently, however, a civil war broke out between Catholics and Protestants in Ireland; a Catholic rebellion took place in 1798, a British force was sent to Ireland and the rebellious Catholics were defeated. The British regained their hold on Ireland, and Pitt initiated bills in both Parliaments (Irish and British) to include Ireland in the British Parliament, where Irish representatives would get one hundred seats in the House of Commons and thirty-two seats in the House of Lords (of which twenty-eight would be assigned to peers and four to bishops). In order to convince the Irish to vote for the bill, Pitt made numerous promises of peerages to members of the Irish Parliament, adding the further promise that Catholic Irish representatives could also enter the British Parliament. The bill was passed in the Irish Parliament, which ceased to exist on 1 January 1801. The bill also passed in the British Parliament, but without the proviso which would have enabled Irish

Catholics to be elected to Parliament. Pitt was forced to renege on this promise because George III was in vehement opposition to it; the king claimed that such a proviso would constitute a violation of the oath he took upon his coronation to fight for the Protestant faith. *In this light, it can be said that religion had thus became part of the British national identity – a sense of nationality connected with the Britons' religious heritage.*

CHAPTER FOUR

The Nineteenth Century CE and the World Wars

By the nineteenth century, Britain had become one of the most affluent nations in Europe. This was a result of the growth of capitalization and industrialization sweeping through the continent at the time, coupled with England's control of the sea. In effect, the period saw Britain's wealthy and affluent become even wealthier, and the commoners poorer. The population also increased significantly; large industries and mechanized-farm owners and managers became richer due to the industrialization boom, while laborers and factory workers were getting poorer and cottage industries were on the decline. During the Victorian period (1837–1901 CE), the British economy flourished as the British Empire expanded its protectorates and colonies, especially in Africa and Asia. In 1815, Britain had suffered from a surfeit of poverty, ignorance, filth and disease. Jeremy Bentham was aged sixty-seven years in 1815; he was an influential legal figure and succeeded in bringing about reform of the legal and judicial system. The poet Shelley (1792–1822 CE) was another critic of the political system; in his poems, he called upon the British to overthrow the evil rule to which they were subjected.

Towards the end of George III's reign, the king suffered from insanity, deafness and blindness; his son and regent, George, ruled in his name and public resentment grew. In 1817, there was a case of the government causing the death and injury of several citizens who came out for a peaceful protest. In the ensuing tense atmosphere, a group of people plotted to assassinate the entire cabinet at dinner; the plot was discovered just in time and the conspirators were hanged. In 1820, George III died and was succeeded on the throne by his son, George IV (reigned 1820–30 CE), who was no more popular than his father.

In 1822, Lord Castlereagh, the leader of the House of Commons, committed suicide. So widespread was public hatred for the government that, as his body was transported through the streets of London, the funeral carriage was greeted by onlookers with shouts of joy. Thereafter, a new cabinet was appointed (1822–27 CE) where George Canning served as foreign minister. He won the enthusiastic trust of politicians and the public alike; many in Britain thought he was the only man capable of saving the country. He appointed two prominent people to key positions: Robert Peel and William Huskisson. Huskisson and Canning are considered to be the founders of the second British Empire; this is because of their policies towards the inhabitants of the colonies, whereby they gave their produce priority over that of any other country and promoted their equality with that of the Britons in Britain. In 1824, the Combinations Acts were repealed; these acts were such that employers were allowed to maltreat their workers because the legislations prevented them from voicing discontent over wages. This development was possible thanks to the effort of a simple tailor, Francis Place, and it pointed to a far-reaching change within British society.

The Popularity of Kings (William IV replacing George IV)

In 1830, the unpopular George IV died, leaving the throne to his brother, William IV, who was popular with the British. This year saw profound changes in British internal politics as a result of revolutions that took place in France and in Belgium. The Belgians successfully rebelled against the king of Holland and his Dutch government, generating debate in the House of Lords on changing the system of government in Britain. Wellington declared himself in favor of this idea, but it was unpopular among the British public, who were proud of their unique constitution. The public response to the prime minister's unpopular stand came in the same year, when general elections were held in which Wellington was not returned to office – an expression of the power that public opinion wielded in that period.

Queen Victoria and her Role in Government

Queen Victoria succeeded William IV at his death in 1837. Victoria, niece to William, was at the time eighteen years of age. She was reported to be a politically-shrewd ruler. Her first step was to surround herself with people loyal to her cause; this is perhaps most noted by her appointment of the experienced Melbourne as prime minister. She was also noted for creating an atmosphere where loyalty to the crown was greatly encouraged. When Sir Robert Peel replaced Melbourne, he put forward policies that went a long way to strengthen the British economy. He favored free trade and a reduction of customs duties, and adhered to the economic theories of Adam Smith. Peel put his policies into effect gradually. He defined three customs levels – the lowest for raw materials, and the highest for foreign-made products which did not require processing in Britain. The year 1852 saw the election of the Whig government and, subsequently, the Conservative government. This period marked another stepping stone in the development of the British national polity. Public opinion had become stronger than the prime minister and stronger than the crown. This state of affairs indicates that Britain had become a democracy, despite the fact that a queen was the head of state.

At the beginning of 1906, the Liberals – as the party in power – easily won the elections backed by Irish nationalist support and also that of the Labor Party. This was the period of economic recession, and the trade unions were on the defensive; when they revived, they evinced a clear aggressiveness. In the beginning, the trade unions only offered skilled laborers membership. By 1880, however, acceptance of unskilled laborers expanded and, by 1889, they were successful in a strike proclaimed by London's dock workers. Due to low dues, unions could only provide financial assistance during a strike at best (with no insurance, etc.), so they recruited more members, reaching 2 million and became more politically influential. The unions adopted socialist ideas, giving rise to practical demands such as an eight-hour workday. In 1906, a more moderate version of socialism appeared in Britain and was successfully adopted. The Liberals promoted legislation that would bring about the transfer of relatively-large agricultural tracts (unprofitable due to the import of cheap wheat from the United States and Russia) from estate owners into the hands of small farmers. The latter would be able to till the land and grow other crops more profitable than wheat since they did not have to compete with cheap foreign imports. An Act passed in 1892 failed to have the desired effect, because estate owners refused to sell their land. Therefore, another Act was passed in 1907; this time, the central government was made responsible for implementing the laws, and it succeeded in forcing the estate owners to sell.

A sense of internal unification is a precondition for the formation of a nationality. The British political system and the expansion of the British Empire would thus seem to have constituted some of the seeds from which the British national identity grew. A description of the expansion of the British Empire is thus a description of one of the components which helped to bring about the emergence of the British nationality.

With respect to the Boers in South Africa, who had surrendered to the British under the agreement of 1902 and were now under British rule, the Liberal government decided not to grant them partial home rule (as had been the case with the rebellious American colonies). Instead, they granted them full home rule in a new Union of South Africa that was established, in 1910, as a dominion of the British Empire.

In India, the British were of the opinion that both pro-independence movements (Hindu and Muslim) were not suitable enough to bring about an autonomous government because of their low level of education. Therefore, the British authorities encouraged educated Indians to join the British government system in India. In the end, supreme power lay in the hands of the British Parliament.

Britain in World War I

The assassination of Archduke Ferdinand and his wife on 28 June 1914, in Sarajevo, was the trigger that set off World War I. The assassination was as a result of conflict between Austria, Russia, Greece and Turkey, amongst other nations in the region. Britain, until 1914, sat on the fence as they were undecided, both at government and public level, about whether to enter the war or to remain neutral. France, one of the foremost British allies, decided it for them by entering the war. Britain had no choice but to follow, reasoning that the power balance in Europe was now under threat and would be more so if a French defeat should occur.

England's bulk participation in the war was expended on checkmating Germany's invasion of Bulgaria by establishing a stable line of defense on the Aisne River. The British and the French were now besieging Germany and the neutral states on its borders, and blockading Germany's overseas colonies (which Britain gradually conquered). In the spring of 1918, the Germans were able to reinforce their troops on the French front but, shortly thereafter, a million American soldiers began to stream in to France. The US had entered the war in the previous year, after a number of American ships had been sunk by the Germans. This constituted a major change to the stalemate on the French-German front, which was supported by a British naval blockade of Germany. These actions resulted in the inevitable fall of the Axis powers: in October and November 1918, the troops of Britain, France, the United States, Italy and the British dominions overcame Turkey, Austria-Hungary and Germany – in that order, and in three campaigns.

Ireland

The Irish, by consensus, refrained from raising nationalist demands during World War I. But, as soon as the war came to an end, they began to demand independence, based on their ancient Celtic heritage which Irish nationalists considered to be the mark of their uniqueness. The government, for its part, offered broad home rule (but not complete independence), with assurances on protecting the rights of the Protestants in the six northern counties. In an assembly convened in Dublin (1919), they declared themselves a Constituent Assembly and announced the establishment of an independent Irish state. In the course of time, all signs of British sovereignty were eradicated in a process which ended in 1937, and Ireland became completely independent, to the chagrin of the British government – which, however, did not consider taking military action on the matter.

From the First to the Second World War

The reparations imposed on Germany after World War I exceeded its ability to pay, and it could pay only with goods produced by its industries. Over time, Germany could no longer afford to pay and this led to an invasion by France, where they seized goods, coal from the German mines, and industrial plants.

In 1933, the Nazi regime that had assumed power in Germany announced that they would not make any further payment towards the German debt.

The Nazi party withdrew from membership in the League of Nations and began to rearm, arguing that the Allies had not disarmed as agreed. In response, in 1936, Britain expanded its armed forces and their armament, especially in the Royal Air Force. In 1934, the Germans signed a mutual non-aggression pact with Poland. In 1938, Nazi Germany occupied Austria, and annexed it two years after a failed coup. In March 1939, Germany sent troops into Czechoslovakia and occupied the entire country (not only the Sudeten region) except for a small area which Hitler decided to annex to Hungary. At that moment, British public opinion finally awoke to the cry 'Hitler must be stopped!', reinforced by martial speeches by both Chamberlain and the French premier. The Soviet Union, which at this time refused to side with France and Britain, entered into a mutual non-aggression treaty with Germany, which was signed and made public on 21 August 1939.

On 3 September 1939, France and Britain declared war on Germany. The Germans, on the other hand, captured Denmark and Norway, and began a naval war in which German submarines sank British merchant vessels. The Germans were unable to invade England thanks to the efficient preparations Britain had made in the buildup to the war.

On 22 June 1941, the Germans invaded the Soviet Union on a broad front. Britain thus gained an ally, the American lend-lease program was expanded, and both Americans and British equipped the Soviets in order to enhance their ability to repulse the Germans. On 7 December 1941, the Japanese attacked the American fleet at Pearl Harbor. According to a pre-existing agreement with the Americans, the British automatically joined the war against Japan; America, as a result, was now at war with Germany. This, according to Lunt's[3] assessment (which is not supported in the present volume), marked the turning point of the war in the Soviet Union, in North Africa and in the Pacific Ocean in favor of the Allies (the United States, Britain, the Soviet Union and their allies).

In 1943, the Allies invaded Sicily and, on September 3 of that year, the invaders entered mainland Italy. On 6 June 1944, Allied forces landed in Normandy, France. Paris was liberated on August 25; Belgium and part of Holland were liberated soon after. On August 15, the Allies landed on the shores of the French Riviera. The German forces in Europe surrendered on 4 May 1945; Japan surrendered too, on 14 August 1945, after two atomic bombs were dropped on its cities.

During the war, the British showed their greatness of spirit in that they showed great cohesion and postponed all their disputes until after the war had ended. This behavior is an indication of the dominant importance of the British national identity. Unlike France, the inhabitants proved brave and spirited in war, and were prepared to suffer and to continue to resist the Ger-

---

3   Lunt, W. E. *History of England*, 4th edition. New York, Evanston and London: Harper and Row, 1928, 1957.

mans. The present volume takes the position that of prime importance are the actions of the public masses and the armed forces.

The Road to Recovery, 1945–55 CE

In the decade following World War II, the British underwent a difficult period of reconstruction in which they advanced from a situation of crisis to one of stability and progress. This process involved a change in government and social and economic experimentation, including rationing, nationalization, government involvement in the economy at the private sector's expense, and a subsequent gradual disengagement from such involvement.

The following parliamentary elections saw the Labor party elected. The Labor Party proposed a platform which encompassed nationalization of the means of production and government supervision. In this period, up to about 20 percent of the country's industries were nationalized; industries that were not nationalized were placed under government supervision – actions that more or less continued the policy of supervision that had been in effect during the war. Britain's survival as an independent state, it was agreed, depended on raising production and reducing consumption.

By 1950, government supervision had become so pervasive that the public began to grumble. Labor's majority was expected to become too small to rule effectively; and indeed, in the elections of October 1951, the Conservatives won a small majority and Churchill once again became prime minister – a post that he retained until he received a knighthood on 6 April 1955, whereupon he handed over the post of prime minister to his fellow Conservative, Anthony Eden.

Empire and Foreign Affairs in the Years 1945–55 CE

In the years 1945–55 CE, Britain lost its imperial possessions as part of a worldwide process to which World War II gave added impetus. The imperial powers voluntarily (or due to a lack of choice) disengaged from their holdings abroad, which they could no longer afford to retain. With regard to this assessment of Lunt's, it should be noted that this trend coexisted with the British tendency (mentioned above) to give freedom to their more advanced dominions.

From this point on (as described by John Richard Green[4] in his *A Short History of the English People*), Britons underwent a quiet internal revolution in which their splendid isolation in resisting the dominant might of Germany in Europe diminished within the span of a few short years to their dependence upon the power of the United States and that of the other non-Com-

---

4   Green, John Richard. *A Short History of the English People*. London: Dent and Sons, 1962.

munist Europeans in order to withstand the Communist forces which were threatening Europe in general, and thus Britain became as a part of Europe.

From the pinnacle of a first-rate power, Britain now became a secondary player subordinate to the truly great superpowers. When, in 1940, the British had stood alone against Germany, they had possessed a world empire comprising the entire Commonwealth of Nations as well as the British colonies. Now, they had to search for a greater power to which they would be subservient; the available choices were the United States of America and the countries of the European Community – in fact, the former choice proved unviable. *However, it should be noted that both in the glory of war and in the following everyday struggle with the ills of their economy, the British proved themselves to be a determined and cohesive collective – a real nationality.*

CHAPTER FIVE

Questions of Identity and Belonging

Immigrants and Foreigners in Britain Today

Cesarani[5] viewed the British as a people who dealt with the foreigners in their midst in a stable and non-discriminatory manner compared with other groups in Europe. He opined that this was the case because of the British inherent loyalty or contract-like commitment between the individual and the community in which he resides. He also notes that, in the seventeenth century CE, the debate on nationality was steeped in topics concerning property, religion and sex; this state of affairs continued throughout the eighteenth and nineteenth centuries CE.

The French Revolution, however, aroused a contrary tendency in Britain. It marked the beginning of new views and beliefs amongst the British people. For the first time, themes of the rights and duties of subjects were debated in Britain; in contrast to the old concept of popular sovereignty, there now arose a new idea of the birthright of the British people, which formed the basis for the actions of the reformists. Massive immigration gave rise to the question of who was entitled to citizenship. The issues of citizenship and nationality raised by this immigration were addressed in Parliament; for example, by the Law Proposing Naturalization of the Jews (1753–54 CE), which would have naturalized Jews not born in Britain despite the fact that Protestantism had long been considered to be the foundation stone of British citizenship. Accepting immigrants was a matter of honor for them; this motivation included the assimilation of refugees and émigrés; it was a principle which melded with the expanding British economy and was aided by the fact that the concept of 'Britishness' was not defined by the British naturalization laws.

By 1870, however, the need for the British to compete on the world stage, the loss of their imperial security, mass immigration of Jews in the years 1882–1905 CE, and a rise in unemployment, amongst other things, gave rise to an enhanced sense of Britishness among the public. The people now questioned whether Jews were sufficiently 'British' to participate in elections. These reactions of the British at the level of their national identity were sim-

---

5   Cesarani, David. "The Changing Character of Citizenship and Nationality in Britain", in *Citizenship, Nationality and Migration in Europe*, eds. David Cesarani and Mary Fulbrook, pp. 57–73. London and New York: Routledge, 1996.

ilar to those demonstrated by the Germans and the French when faced with similar situations. This led to legislation being passed to limit immigration to Britain in 1905. In 1914, restrictions were placed upon the movements of aliens, who were required to register with the police. It became increasingly more difficult to become British, as had also been the case with those residents of Britain's dominions who came to live in Britain. At the end of World War II, further restrictions were imposed in the wake of the transformation of the Empire into the Commonwealth.

Cesarani is of the opinion that wars are important factors in shaping a national identity – to the British, their wars were associated with the heroism of white Britons. Ethnic origin, religion, customs and language all contributed towards making it difficult for non-white immigrants to assimilate with the British people; they could thus be kept outside the bounds of the concept of 'Britishness' without any overt reference to race. He argues that citizenship (no less than national identity) equals nationality; the concept of loyal citizenship thus gradually evolved into a sense of the collective uniformity of white citizens.

The present study perceives nationality differently than does Cesarani, who (along with other proponents of state nationality) sees citizenship as a legal status (defined by the laws of each nation-state) that is automatically associated with national identity. However, national identity is an imaginary construct that emerges from the feelings and emotions of members of a group who perceive themselves as belonging to a certain nation – it is thus possible to distinguish between citizenship and nationality. The transition from nationality to citizenship (and vice versa) is a transition between two distinct legal systems: state law and social law. This is a distinction which stands at the center of our PhD thesis[6] that deals with transitions among constitutional rules and principles, which are either denied (a conscious transition whose existence is hidden from the view of others) or hidden (by the person who does the hiding himself), and which belong to three distinct domains: state law, societal law and spiritual law.

The Question of British Nationality and the EU

In Eatwell's[7] view, the unchallenged, conventional British view in the immediate post-World War II period is one of a traditional nationality based upon the heritage of a thousand-year monarchy, seven hundred years of Parliament, an ancient language and culture and a dominant Church. This view became distorted and underwent changes in the years following 1945. It is true that the British did bolster their classical picture by constructing myths around

6   Cohen, Yehuda. *Hidden or Denied Constitutional Rules or Principles*. PhD thesis, Faculty of Law. Jerusalem: The Hebrew University of Jerusalem, 2006.

7   Eatwell, Roger. "Britain", in *European Political Cultures – Conflict or Convergence*, ed. Roger Eatwell, pp. 50–68. London and New York: Routledge, 1997.

it; these myths encouraged them in days of peace and in times of crisis, and even accompanied them in the course of their empire-building. Myths gave direction to their steps, confidence in their mission and justification in their wars against the Spaniards, the French and the Germans – unifying factors that added to the framework of their racial awareness. Their myths were constructed from such diverse elements as religion (Protestantism), Parliament (the idea of its supremacy) and a devilish enemy (which, for a long time, was identified with France). The British persisted in this process and also built myths around their solitary resistance when Nazi Germany had striven to achieve dominance in Europe and beyond, in the dark and portentous days before the Soviet Union and the United States joined the British in their war against the Germans and their allies.

During both the formation of the British Empire and the evolution of the British Commonwealth, the British operated not only from a desire to improve their own economic situation but also held a view of themselves as a chosen people striving for liberty and personal freedom. The British fostered their collective memories of the Viking raids before the Norman invasion (and the Norman invasion itself), thus shaping the essence of British identity. In fact, the British developed a national identity before they became acquainted with liberal trends, and certainly before they encountered Socialism. Their trade unions were moderate, due both to the harmonious political climate that encouraged them to obtain concessions from employers and the German economic and military threat against which all Britons were united – radicalism was inappropriate under these circumstances. During both World Wars, the British were intensely nationalist, as evidenced by their eagerness to fight against the Germans; there were even those (like the coal miners of South Wales) who fought out of a hatred of the Germans, who appeared to them to be no better than animals. Although signs of Socialist combativeness appeared in Britain shortly after the Russian Revolution, these rapidly dissipated.

The British experienced many social developments on issues of homogeneity, consensus and mutual respect from the late 1960s up till the 90s. In Wales and Scotland, there was a growing sense of their separate nationalities although, at the beginning of the 1980s, fully 86 percent of their populations were proud of being British, while only 8 percent claimed not to be proud of that fact. Abundant opposition to 'Englishness' exists today in Wales and Scotland; the economic assistance received from the British treasury has proved unable to stem these feelings.

Eatwell believes that there is no uniform attitude towards either participation in or withdrawal from the European Union; instead of integration with the EU, many Britons prefer to take a distinct and separate British path – especially with respect to issues of their currency and economy. Narin[8] states that the British system is not defined by a written constitution, but is rather the end-product of a gradual evolution of accepted practices. It must be noted

---

8   Nairn, Tom. *The Break-Up of Britain – Crisis and Neo-Nationalism*. London: NLB, 1977.

here that the British system is truly a unique remnant of an ancient regime; this is because the representative democracy currently practiced in Britain is the end result of gradual growth and not the outcome of a decision to adopt a certain system at a given moment, and this system remains till this day in a state of constant flux. Although the British system gave birth to modern constitutionalism, it is not in itself a modern constitutional system. The traits possessed by the British nation (including greater social mobility, individualism, openness, equality, development of personal skills and uncompromising traditional strictness) demonstrate the internal strength of a system based on the intelligentsia and needless of revolution – whether 'from below' or 'from above'. A sense of loyalty to the 'British tribe' is ingrained in Britons in their modern incarnation; the public have a mystical faith in the British system and constitution, in its ability to overcome obstacles and to be victorious in battle. The British public believes that its ruling elite will nurture the populace – British society as a whole trusts its government. Nairn claims that the chances for federal relations between different parts of Britain are very slim. For over two hundred years, the English maintained a lifestyle and a constitution based on conservatives, nobles and liberals, and both the Scots and the Welsh adopted and became assimilated into this society. It can be said that Englishmen feel uncomfortable with their ties to the European Union, feeling that these reduce the stature of the British nation and their formerly imperial status to less than a nation-state.

Peter Leese[9] describes the post-1945 British identity as a collective core of four nationalities, with margins that consist of the Celts and the subsequent races which integrated with them. His depiction is in no way dramatic or political, being based upon a perspective from everyday life. The British, so far, do not appear to have attained a state in which they can envision a British national identity in the context of assimilation with the European Community; nor does the motivation to build a new European national identity appear to exist within Britain today.

The British in the EU: A Summary

British and Norwegian relationships with the EU are described by Robert Geyer[10]. He notes the initial opposition of the British Labor Party and its Norwegian counterpart to membership in the European Community. This resistance began to weaken in the 1980s; at the end of that decade, the British Labor Party decided in favor of membership, while Norway maintained its separate status outside of the Union. However, Geyer stresses that the ideals of a nation-state were not abandoned. The view promulgated by this present volume is that life in Britain proceeds less in accordance with

9   Leese, Peter. *Britain since 1945 – Aspects of Identity*. New York: Palgrave Macmillan, 2006.
10 Geyer, Robert. *The Uncertain Union – British and Norwegian Social Democrats in an Integrating Europe*. Aldershot, England: Ashgate Publishing Company, 1997.

pan- European ideas, but evolves more in line with practices and traditions that existed even when British ideological sympathy favored the neo-liberalism which developed in the Western world. Geyer mentions the motivations that guided the British Labor Party but does not emphasize this unique British path, merely highlighting that the Labor party acted in the interests of its members – a motivation which is not unique to the British. He says that Labor learned from experience at the ballot box that adherence to neo-liberalism, despite its remoteness from the socialist theories it wished to promote, ensured support on election day; whereas the more it moved in the opposite, socialist direction, the worse became its electoral performance.

In light of Ingimundarson's[11] description, together with Geyer's comments on the changes in the social policies of the British Labor Party which made it possible for Britain to enter the European Community, it seems to us that the entrance of Britain into the EC and its activity within the framework of the European Union indicates that British identity has taken precedence over European identity. This state of affairs is similar to British behavior within the framework of their Commonwealth. While the British like to operate in large-scale organizations that wield global influence (and enhance the British economy, the British currency and the prestige of the British Crown), they certainly do not want to shed their British national identity. All of these developments have not changed the basic fact that the British identity supersedes (in British eyes) any other political identity they may possess. Membership of Europe, to a large extent, serves as an instrument to strengthen their British identity – in the assessment of this study, that is the role of the European identity as perceived by the British.

The British National Identity

So, who are the British? No discussion of the British can be brought to a satisfactory conclusion without understanding, or at least defining, who and what the British are, and whom they include. These questions are raised by Hugh Kearney[12] in his volume *The British Isles*. According to his study, the British consist of four 'nations' (English, Scots, Welsh and the people of Northern Ireland), as well as the inhabitants of a number of semi-independent smaller islands (such as the Isle of Man and the Channel Islands) and the non-white immigrants from India, Pakistan, the Caribbean and Africa (who, together, make up about 8 percent of the population). Each of the

---

11 Ingimundarson, Valur. "The American Dimension: Britain, Germany, and the Reinforcement of US Hegemony in Europe in the 1990s", in *Uneasy Allies – British-German Relations and European Integration since 1945*, eds. Klaus Larres with Elizabeth Meehan, pp.165–183. Oxford: Oxford University Press, 2000.

12 Kearney, Hugh. *The British Isles – A History of Four Nations*. Cambridge: Cambridge University Press, 1989, 2006.

aforementioned groups has retained its own unique culture and society – this is especially true of the Muslims and Hindus.

In our eyes, this form of analysis is valid for the EU as well, not just for Britain. In the EU, there are numerous immigrants that do not assimilate into the Christian-European culture. This state of affairs affects many of the groups which make up the European Community, especially in pivotal countries such as France, Germany, Britain and the Netherlands. The picture which thus emerges is of a common Europe-wide force with the power to ensure European cohesion and negate the specific national traits of the EU groups today – and during the future course of twenty-first-century Europe.

The British have preserved their strong sense of nationality, while all other groups within the EU have lost their national sense of political separateness. Linkage to the EU is the only option for the national identity for other groups – the European nationality provided by the European Union is now the only relevant national identity for them. Of all the groups discussed in this series, the British are unique in their robust, inherited, deep-seated, political, separate nationality, which they will not relinquish within the framework of the EU. For that reason, it is obvious that the British commitment to membership of the European Union is not valid. The British will be left with their unique ancient myths – a hard kernel from which the ancient English-British national identity will continue to bloom. No economic benefit conferred by membership of the EU will nullify the vitality and internal liveliness of the British national identity rather than any possible super-European nationality.

Appendix A

Contemporary Political Analysis: The British and their Future within the EU

In the 2014 European Parliamentary elections, the UK Independence Party (UKIP) seriously intended to fulfill its promise of Britain's desertion of the EU, while France's *Front National* seemed to make only a hollow declaration of its intention to leave the union (for elaboration about the French, see www.priestspublishing.com). The UKIP's leaders were consistent with their declared aims and refused to act in any way incompatible with their unique, independent policy. This attitude of the British is no surprise bearing in mind their very nature and nationality as discussed in the chapters of this book. Considering the story of Henry and Becket, the stories of Henry II, Richard I (Lionheart) and the Crusades, and John and the Magna Carta, one may trace in them the foundations of myths together with extensive legal literature that have coalesced over time to unify the English as a nation.

The characteristics of the British nationality are rather heterogenic: the Welsh (1265–84 CE) on their part were able to develop their literature and poetry to such an extent that it surpassed any other European country. Their culture shows the spiritual strength of the Welsh people and demonstrates how a group under irresolvable military pressure seeks relief in literary expression. By this method, the Welsh proved their spiritual vitality and managed to preserve their unique language, although not forever. The Scottish also were united under the rule of Duncan (1034–40 CE) and subsequently his son, Malcolm, who killed Macbeth (Duncan's killer) and became king of Scotland (1057–93 CE), founding a dynasty which ruled the country for some two hundred years and shaped a Scottish national identity.

A solid foundation of British nationality was the method of influencing public opinion through works of literature read by the educated masses, indicating a high level of culture generating political power. It also indicates a measure of internal cohesion on the part of the educated English masses, which in turn made it possible to build a national identity without having to resort to revolutionary methods, befitting the unique English character.

What makes Britain so different today compared to other European groups? It is simply that only the British have a stable nationality that is more precious to them than their European identity. If we consider martyrdom, we see that it has been instrumental in shaping a unique British nationality and, in that sense, alienated them from the rest of Europe. Christian martyrdom took on the form of a special language which evolved in England and which did not necessarily involve sacrificing one's life, but could consist of suffering that contained a message of a great power. Those who suffered in this way were greatly admired. Not all European groups shared this tendency, which emerged among the English. Those unique characteristics took a metamorphosis when Churchill's blood-toil-tears-and-sweat speech inaugurated the period in which the British single-handedly withstood the German attack between June 1940 and June 1941. This period was a clear sign that an intense British nationality had already been forged. This is what gives today's Britons a unique strength which is lacking in other contemporary European groups. This kind of collective strength of mind is not something which the EU would easily be able to digest in its attempt to create a single, uniform, united, European national identity. Britain's full integration into Europe therefore has been incomplete, also because the UK has retained the right to secede from the EU: the UK's entry into the Union was by an Act of Parliament and can be overturned at any time by another Act of Parliament. In this respect, the British differ from the other groups which have joined the EU without retaining a legal avenue to abandon the European wagon.

The English sense of nationality has greatly been influenced by the country's foreign policies over the course of their history. For events pertaining to the Hundred Years' War in France, the heroic deeds of their Black Prince in this popular war, fought by adventure-loving volunteers, provided the basis of powerful national folk myths that gave shape to the sense of collective English nationality. Such myths constitute the building blocks of a national identity – defining the moment when a collective mass within a group begins to take part in its country's politics – on the condition, however, that disruptive internal forces are not dominant. Another case for the British separatism can also be traced to their own unique acceptance of the socialist trend that generated demonstrations and destruction in other European countries in 1848 (which became known as the European 'Spring of Nations'). In Britain, this spirit of reform was of a positive and constructive nature. Britain came out of the period as a beacon of constructive society, as an island of stability. Britain took then a unique, more constructive, path as it has done in former centuries. Indeed, the British traveled a quite different road compared to continental groups as was found in an all-European academic research project into the formation and dissolution of European nationalities and the formation of one European super-nationality. This research was published in a series of ten volumes about the histories and national identities of ten European groups (the French, Germans, Spanish, Italians, Dutch, Polish, Hungarians, Bulgarians, Swedes and British) over the last 1,500 years. This e-book is a synopsis of the volume about the British. For details, see Appendix B and www.priestspublishing.com.

The British are perhaps the most favored candidates of all European groups for the emergence of a national and collective spirit, as well as a cultural distinction. This is because of their unique position on a group of islands – a position that affected a sense of self-worth upon them.

All those factors played a part in the emergence of the British strong self-esteem, and can explain the resultant economy that reflected British strength and endurance as well as cultural dominance, as shown by the dissemination of their language and culture worldwide. The British indeed nurtured and esteemed their national identity, as embodied in Britain's royal dynasty that symbolizes their long imperial tradition. Those unique characteristics of the British can explain the unique results of the 2014 EU parliamentary elections in Britain.

Relying on the above analysis, one may conclude that the British value their own national identity much more than their European belonging; thus, the results of their expected 2016/7 referendum are foreseen to herald Britain's departure from the EU._

Appendix B

A Post- or Super-Nationality in the European Union

The Series Preface

On 26 May 2014, elections for the European Parliament took place, and Europe was shocked by the success of right-wing parties proposing secession from the European Union (EU). The most successful party in that capacity was Britain's UK Independence Party, closely followed by France's National Front, led by Marine le Pen.

This series of ten volumes about ten European groups – the Germans, the French, the Spanish, the Italians, the British, the Dutch, the Polish, the Hungarians, the Bulgarians and the Swedes – provides a fresh view of each of these groups, and consequently may shed light on the EU and its future political and sociological prospects.

The volume dealing with **the French** analyzes the course of French history since the thirteenth century CE onward, searching the depths of the French collective memory and the motifs that dominate their behavior to this day. It touches the rich history of the French from the One Hundred Years' War with England to the Black Death, the French Revolution, the Bonaparte era, the World Wars and thereafter. The volume's main findings are that the French had adopted a motif of rioting in the wake of terrible traumas dated back to the thirteenth century; thus the 'French Revolution' was a mere riot which later on was mythicized to seize ideological dominance in Europe; in light of these motifs, the French will probably provide the EU with ideological leadership.

The Germans, with their loyalties split between the different German states, are seen as not having a true common nationality until Adolf Hitler came to power, whereupon a theory of race was adopted that provided all Germans with a common long, imaginary history. That national feeling was lost after Germany's defeat in World War II; it was lost partly due to the shame of the Holocaust that derived from that racial theory, and partly because they were happy to share with other European groups a perception that the two horrible 'World Wars' were superfluous conflicts between groups of the same family – people who had the same culture, traditions and history, who shared similar beliefs, futures and enemies, who wished to cooperate politically and economically. The volume's main finding is that dominance and a leadership role have always been a German objective even when they themselves treasure no nationality; the Germans will certainly continue to aspire to those objectives within the EU.

The height of **Spanish** civilization was reached during the period of Muslim rule. The Spanish attained their 'Golden Age' in the tenth to the thirteenth centuries CE. But while Muslim religious tolerance made the Spanish the intellectual leaders of Europe and the Mediterranean, the opposite happened under Catholic religious fanaticism, which led to economic ruin, only temporarily relieved by the achievements of imperial conquest. For the Spanish, European integration is stronger than any Spanish nationality. They may thus become a constructive component in the developing European national identity.

The **Italians** had been divided into North and South for many generations since the Roman era. Their experiences with foreign invaders and the lack of strong local government led them to perceive that help only derives from the family; that explains why apparently family-like organizations like the Mafia and the Fascist regime based upon family-like strings were trusted more than any form of government – including the EU. So the Italians, generally speaking, do not provide a source of support for any political regime, but are also unlikely to secede from the EU; they have no better alternative political frame.

The **Dutch** settled the coastline where rivers from Central Europe flow into the North Sea. They were exposed to winds and sea waves, learned from the forces of nature how to create lakes, make windmills, exploit sea and wind for the construction of ships, for developing commerce, for joining sea and river shipping, and for creating an industry based on wind energy. The main difficulties facing the Dutch were mostly the forces of nature; thus they developed a practical approach to overcoming obstacles. The Dutch uplifted themselves by the practical resolution of difficulties, while other countries were preoccupied with human rivalries. The unique Dutch way of life was not seriously threatened by the German occupation along World War II, and the Dutch cooperated with the German occupation force – thus showing their status as a non-national group, since their cherished fortune was their special way of life rather than their political independence. In the absence of coherent political national aims, the Dutch have no real nationality; they would be happy to take part in the integration of the EU.

The **Polish** national history, feelings and struggles are millennia-long, mostly contained within the borders of a Polish state, but this was a quasi-nationality shared only by the nobility and wealthy citizens. When Poland's independence was achieved at the end of 1918, an inner change evolved and the majority of Poles embraced politics. After World War II, the Communist regime exhibited a dignified national stance, supported by the majority of

Poles, and its political acts showed the existence of a real Polish nationality. In the 1990s, Poland accepted a European identity. The Polish were keen to be accepted by the EU and will not probably deny their membership of Europe; this European identity they own is truly stronger than their imaginary Polish national feeling.

The Hungarians (Magyars), based upon a group of tribes who came to Europe from Central Asia around 896 CE, settled in the Tisza valley in the Carpathian basin. About 955 they accepted Christianity and, in 1222, Hungarian King Andrew II was forced to give the nobility a letter of rights. Until the end of World War I, most Hungarians, including peasants and town citizens, believed in a partnership with the Austrians and common ownership of the Austro-Hungarian Empire. Gradually, from the end of the nineteenth century until the conclusion of World War I, the peasants and other commoners crystallized Hungarian national feelings and political awareness. After World War I and through World War II, the Hungarians preserved their nationality – until the 1990s, when the opportunity arose to join the EU. Hungary determined to take the European route; Hungary being a small country with limited economic strength, while the European Union was a huge economic entity, richer and more modern than themselves. Therefore, they gave up their sovereignty to the EU; they are today more European than Hungarian.

The Bulgarians are comprised of two different ethnic groups, each having different cultural attributes – Slavic settlers who excelled as farmers and Bulgarian tribes who excelled in fighting. In 866 CE, Bulgaria accepted Christianity, and soon after developed a unique religious attitude that derived from Bulgarian myths together with a high level of literacy throughout the Bulgarian community – something that no other European group or community could boast. Bulgaria's decision to join the EU evolved from their ancient attitude identifying with Europe; therefore, the series finds that the Bulgarians are a positive element within the EU.

The Swedes never possessed a real feudal system with their lands not fertile enough. Swedish peasants were mostly free and, in 1434, gained real political status for the first time when they mutinied in the southern provinces, led by a low-level noble, and achieved the establishment of a *Riksdag* (parliament). Wars and strife enabled more educated Swedes to become politically active and strong, thus developing a Swedish national identity within the wider population. Although armed with a strong sense of nationality and political reckoning on the continent, the Swedes were quick to realize that they could not maintain an independent role in European 'jungle politics' and their usual attempt at neutrality could even prove dangerous so, after much hesitation, they jumped into the European 'swimming pool'. They now feel very comfortable floating there, and would prefer to stay there in the future, adapting to a European nationality.

The British have a long history, full of uniting myths. In this they differ from the Germans. The English and the British allowed broad classes of people to participate in the political process, giving British nationality a wide base of 'a nation in power' in the same sense as 'a nation in arms'; this power is expressed daily in their parliamentary House of Commons. Historically, there is a connection between British expansion and empire building and British expansion by way of membership of the EU. In our series survey, Britain was found to be the only country with a vitality and strength greater than the tendency towards pan-European integration within the EU. That result is important for the proposed national referendum in 2016/7 regarding Britain's membership of the EU. The British are the only group in the series unwilling to give up their specific nationality to become full partners in EU integration if and when the EU's citizens come to constitute one united super-nationality.

www.ingramcontent.com/pod-product-compliance
Lightning Source LLC
Chambersburg PA
CBHW070617290526
45790CB00002B/932